A
A BOAT...
AND YOU

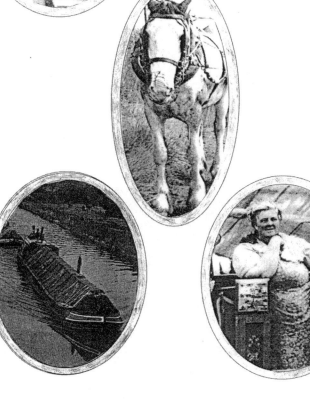

2

A HORSE, A BOAT, AND YOU

A TRIBUTE TO GEORGE AND ANNE WAIN

By
ALICE LAPWORTH

ISBN 978-0-9564536-4-8

First published in Great Britain in 2012

SGM Publishing
47 Silicon Court, Shenley Lodge, Milton Keynes MK5 7DJ
www.sgmpublishing.co.uk

In memory of my Parents, George and Anne Wain:

Dad's dream was to have a horse boat of his own, and a wife and family to share it with him. This proved to be a hard life but a happy one, working and living on the canals.

In this book I will try to explain what it was really like being a child growing up into a world of hard work and long hours, living in cramped conditions.

ROOTS

It was a hard life, working on the canals. But many people had no option – when the First World War was over, it was all they knew, their only source of income, as it was for my mother's parents, George and Annie Evans. They worked a horse-boat all their lives – they lived in Tunstall, but their work for Mersey Weavers took them from the Staffordshire Potteries to the ports of Manchester, Weston Point and Runcorn, carrying cargoes of wheat, coal, china clay, flint, sugar, and so on.

This must have been particularly hard for Grandma, a Yorkshire woman born and bred, who had come off the land to work with her husband on the canals. When they first got married, Granddad had tried to teach her to steer the boat while he walked with the horse by placing a lump of cheese on one side of the cabin top and a piece of bread on the other – at each bend in the canal he would then shout back to her "Hold to cheese" or "Hold to bread". Unfortunately this method proved unsuccessful – as hunger took over the bread and cheese would get eaten and so from then on she had to trust to luck!

Life had to go on as they travelled, and indeed bringing up their family of ten, five girls and five boys, must have been a struggle. They were Anne, Phyllis, Alice, Annie (my Mam) and Madge, and George, Jack, Jim, Bill and Albert. They lost the eldest two, George and Anne, to epilepsy at a young age – and fatalities were common, as they experienced with Madge who

Grandma Annie Evans in her cottage. The picture at her elbow is of Grandad George Evans

died at the age of seven in Etruria when the horse reared and threw her to her death.

The children didn't have it easy either; they had to work alongside their parents, and equally as hard. Long days, with little sleep in cramped conditions. Schooling was limited to how long they stayed in one town, just a few days here and there, and not all the children were able to attend school at all. Annie and Phyllis had no schooling, but all the others had. My mother's two remaining sisters married into the same boating family – Alice married Reg Barnett, and Phyllis married Rafe Barnett. The boys were not interested in the canals and when they were old enough they left and settled in Tunstall, as did my grandmother.

My Mam was left to work with her father, working for the Anderton Company boats. She always told us how elaborately painted the cabins were on the Anderton Company horse-boats; flowers decorated every corner, even the soap 'ole. On the inner cabin walls she could remember painted farmyard scenes.

Mam spent her time tending the horse and tramping alongside it, from a very early age. As she became tired of walking she used to attach a boot onto a piece of string and let it dangle from the line behind the horse – the noise it made clattering along together with a slap on the rump was enough to make the horse believe she was still following him, but instead she was on the boat! That was a regular trick of the horse-boaters, to keep the horse from slowing down or stopping. To quicken the pace all you had to do was throw a small piece of coal at its rump.

The horse was a constant companion on the many long and lonely journeys, especially when negotiating a tunnel. Granddad would have to leg the boat through the tunnel, and Mam would follow the towpath with the horse over the tunnel and wait at the other end for her Dad and the boat to come through. This could be in the dead of night, so Mam depended on the horse for a bit of company.

You got to know your horse, even recognising the sound of its hooves as it clip-clopped through a bridge 'ole. I suppose you could say it became part of the family, and as such it too had to be chastised when it was out of order. Many a one was pushed into the cut to teach it a lesson and get it back in line!

As they travelled along Mam used to collect all the pieces of rope she could find and let them dry on the cabin top. When enough had been collected, her Dad used to take it to a place in Runcorn and exchange it for money; the rope pieces were used to make more rope. Mam was eighteen when war broke out, hearing Winston Churchill's announcement on the wireless while at Tunstall wharf, but life for her went on as before, until it was arranged for her to meet up with a certain George Wain, whom she had known of all her life, but never met.

Grandma Evans was against the relationship from the start. She never liked the Wain family, carrying on a family feud which had started generations before them, and forbade George from coming to their home. It came to a point, after a lot of arguing, when Grandma hit Annie, and that was when she decided to leave home and went to Big Lock, Middlewich, to meet up with George. Her mother didn't speak to her for a long time, and even reported her to Mersey Weavers for being too young to work for them, although she was twenty at the time. Her objective was to get Annie back, because she could handle the horse while Granddad steered the boat. He eventually gave up boating following an incident when Alice was lucky to avoid

Grandad Jack Wain serving during the First World War

serious injury; she'd accidentally got herself caught up in the horse's straps while they were negotiating the top lock at Stoke.

Grandma and Granddad Wain also had to earn a living on the canals, and they were employed by Mersey Weavers. They were known to the boat people as the watercress boats, because of the amount of water they took on! Travelling on one of these boats used to make your arms ache because you were constantly pumping water out, but the pay was better than other firms so you put up with the discomfort. They had three sons, George (my Dad), Bill and Jim, and two girls, Lizzie and Francis. They lost two other children, a boy and a girl, who died of meningitis.

George Wain and Annie Evans first spoke to one another as George was shovelling china clay out of one of Joe Wain's boats at Mersey Weavers' depot in Tunstall. It was at Westport

11

Lake, Longport, sitting with Annie watching a horse-boat go by, that he said:

'That's what I want – a horse, a boat, and you!' He'd have been about 17 or 18, and quite sweet on Annie – that was to be the start of a long, hardworking but happy relationship.

George, when he was old enough, moved down to London to work for British Waterways as a mate, where he stayed for about five years. He worked with many boat people - one of the captains he worked with was Jack Lane. Grandma Wain arranged for George, who was then twenty-five years of age, to come back up north to meet Annie again, a mere slip of a lass at twenty, who was still working with her Dad.

My Dad, George Wain, had been away from the potteries for a while, working on the London Road, when his Mam sent that message to call him back. He'd been as mate with Charlie Lane for a while, then he went with George Radford, but she called him back because she said that Annie Evans, my Mam, was still single, and she wanted them to get married. And they did marry, of course.

He had a single horse boat then, with Mersey Weavers – they were wooden boats, and we had to keep throwing water over the cabins, to keep them sealed up tight. If you didn't, they'd dry out, and then when it rained you'd get water coming in all over you. They had that horse boat all through the war, until about 1946, and even then he didn't want to get rid of the horse.

George and Annie decided to marry, and the date was fixed, but before the day came around, unfortunately, George's mother passed away. Annie had managed to save a small amount of money, and it was enough to cover the funeral expenses with a little remaining, but they could do no more than use the same funeral clothes for their wedding. They had no money for new shoes, so cardboard insoles had to make do to protect their feet as their old shoes were worn through. But get married they did – on September 3rd 1941 they tied the knot at Stoke registry office.

So George got his horse, his boat and his Annie, but it wasn't easy. Their worldly goods were few and far between, even having to share their one and only plate for meals. Annie thought nothing of this, because her mother used to serve up their meals on one plate, divided into equal portions, but for George the temptation was too great. The first time Annie served breakfast for the two of them on the same plate, he ate the lot; then of course there was a row, but it didn't last for long.

Their trips from the potteries to Weston Docks would take them via the Anderton Lift and onto the River Weaver. Mam never liked the rivers, so she did no more than walk the horse along the main road from Anderton Lift to Runcorn, through the centre of Runcorn town and on to Weston Point, where she would meet up with Dad and the boat, who'd been towed by one of the river boats to the docks. When they were working, they never liked to wear coats, whatever the weather. A heavy coat was bulky and could get in the way; if it got caught on anything, like the paddle-gear at a lock, it could easily tip you in the water.

George always called Annie 'Shaver', because her father was Irish, – you don't hear it so much now, but it was a common term for the Irish then. But she had her own back! He liked to keep the white lines on the boat well scrubbed and clean, and he always used Flash on them, so 'Flash' it was.

Their first son, Denis, was born on May 2nd 1942, at Grandma Evans' home in Tunstall. Poor Mam was in labour from Saturday to Saturday before he made his appearance.

When Denis was three, he developed epileptic fits, which frightened Mam – it was Dad who had to deal with him when the fits came on. By the age of five he was still suffering from them. But one day they happened to be moored up near to Dad's family when Denis had a bad fit; Dad was in the stable tending to the horse so Granddad Wain managed to get Denis on his knee. Granddad was smoking a pipe, and did no more than gently blow the smoke into Denis's face – whether it was coincidence or what we'll never know, but he has never had another fit from that day to this.

Vera, their second child, was born in 1943, and entered the world with a hair-raising experience! Mam was at the pictures watching a scary film about Count Dracula's wife, and that promptly started her labour pains. When baby Vera entered the world her hair was standing on end, and that earned her the nickname of Count Dracula's Wife.

My entry into the world came next, and again it wasn't without incident. Mam and Dad had tied up not far from

14

Grandma Evans' home in Tunstall; Mam attended a hospital appointment and was told the birth was a fortnight away. Whilst visiting her parents, she decided to have a drink of Andrews Liver Salts, and on the way back to the boat she started with labour pains. Dad was away helping his sister on her boat, so Mam summoned the help of her two brothers who happened to be fishing nearby. They brought Grandma back, but because she was rather a large woman, she couldn't get into the back cabin, so the midwife was sent for.

As you can imagine, there was not a lot of room in the back cabin for what was about to happen – Mam was arranged on the bed, the opposite way to the way you would normally sleep so that the midwife could tend to her nether regions. I weighed in, in a nappy on a fishing scale, at eleven pounds! When Dad returned he was surprised to find Mam in bed, and even more surprised when he was presented with his new daughter, who he promptly took away to show off to his sister Lizzie.

Their life went on, ferrying loads of all descriptions from the ports to the potteries, often travelling nonstop from Harecastle to Manchester docks. The canals played an important part in the war because they were a means of carrying supplies to our troops who were training in the Potteries – Dad, being exempt from the army, was one of the boatmen needed to carry these essential supplies of food and coal. The runs were not without incident – on one occasion Mam, then eight and a half months pregnant with her fourth child, was walking alongside the horse as she always did when Dad, on the boat with the other three children, spotted a German bomber coming over from Ellesmere Port. The plane took a run along the canal straight for them; Dad shouted for Mam to get under the horse – there was nowhere else for her to go. Luckily one of our planes from Anderton intercepted and chased the intruder away, and it was eventually shot down over Weston Point.

It was common for the enemy planes to follow the route of the canals, often aided on a cloudless night by the moonlight casting a silvery sheen on the water. They led them right into the hearts of the cities, and the other way to the ports, both prime targets because of the disruption that could be caused to industry. You couldn't hide your boat anywhere, so the boat people were constantly in danger. Little if any mention is made of the part that the boat people played in the war, constantly in danger and struggling to survive on meagre rations, in cramped conditions.

On occasions we had a cargo of horse manure to take from the stables at the depot in the Potteries to a farmer's field at Malkin's Bank. This wasn't a pleasant task, as you can imagine, and Dad had to blank off the cargo area to stop the manure seeping through into the cabin. When the load was emptied, every board had to be scrubbed, as did our clothes and us as well!

It became increasingly difficult for my parents to purchase food and cigarettes due to the rationing restrictions. Mam on one occasion went into a shop for some bananas for us and was given one – the rest were being kept for the shopkeeper's regulars. We could never become any shopkeeper's 'regulars' because we were never in the same town or village long enough to qualify. Even after the war, whenever we went into shops we had to wait until the regulars were served before the shopkeeper would attend to us. If we were carrying coal, small quantities would be exchanged for potatoes or anything else we could use for a meal. Dad would keep a couple of chickens – he sent George and I into the hold one day to catch one of these chickens so it could be prepared for the evening meal. What a performance! Neither of us had any idea of what we were doing and Dad had a good laugh at the antics of the two of us trying.

My Uncle Jim, Dad's youngest brother, came to live with us at the age of fifteen, and he used to keep pigeons for the same purpose. Even water had to be begged for – I can remember taking the watercan to the houses and having to ask them for water because there were no taps along the way as there are nowadays. Taps and toilets were later installed at the depots.

During the war women were taken on to operate the some of the boats in place of the men who had gone to join the forces. These women were paid by the government and by the waterways, but my mother and other mothers like her worked for no wage at all. It was expected of them to tend to the butty while their husbands manned the motor, and they had a family to attend to, washing to do and meals to cook. It brings a smile to my face when I hear modern-day boat owners say they're worn out after boating for a few hours – I wonder how they would have coped with what working boaters had to do to survive!

George and Jim Wain at Tyseley, Birmingham, 1950s

My sister Anne was born in May 1946 at Tunstall. As a child she was very poorly with pneumonia and meningitis; I can remember my Mam and Dad and my aunts taking it in turn to sit with her day and night until she got over the crisis period.

Dad had had enough of the canals at this stage. He acquired the tenancy of his father's house in Cocklebell Row, Tunstall, across the canal from Grandma Evans. There was no electric in the house and we made do with paraffin lamps that hung from the ceiling; the drinking water came from an outside pump which we shared with our neighbours. He took a job stoking the

18

furnaces in the Pot Banks, where they manufactured quarry tiles – I remember taking his sandwiches to him at lunchtime and sitting with him in the fresh air while he ate them. He used to be soaking wet with perspiration – what a difference it was being cooped up in such heat after the freedom he had on the cut. It was while we lived in Cocklebell Row that the next addition to the family arrived: George, in 1947.

George Wain on the Nuneaton, at Hillmorton on the Oxford Canal, with his son David, Alice's brother, on the butty Titania.

In addition to looking after the family, Mam took in washing for the passing boat people and would have it washed and ironed ready for them on their return journey. She also found time to clean at Mrs Evans' chip shop in Tunstall. In the end the stoking job proved too much for Dad's health, and back to the canals he went.

19

During the next ten years three more of my brothers were born – Dave, John and Ray. The youngest of the family, Alan, was born in London, but Mam's health was not so good during this pregnancy and she had to stay in hospital for five months before he was born. Dad, Vera and I carried on the day-to-day working and looking after the family while Mam was in hospital.

Alice's youngest brother Alan, pictured at Tyseley in Birmingham at about three years old.

LIFE WITH MAM & DAD

When I was little, we used to carry all kinds of things. Very often it would be china clay, we'd go to Weston Point to load, and then up the lift (Anderton) onto the main line to go to the potteries. Then maybe back empty to Manchester where we'd load flour in the docks, straight out of the ships. That would go to a big bread and cake factory at Longport – we liked that trip, because once we'd unloaded we'd usually get given some cakes! Longport was our main base, and we'd have gravel loaded there sometimes, for Old Trafford in Manchester. I didn't like that, because it would be brought in trucks, which they'd back up to the boat and tip it in – Dad had to be inside the boat, to shovel it out level, and that scared me.

Then sometimes we'd go to Sidaway Colliery, to load coal which had to go to a salt factory in Stoke, just below the second lock where they had their own little basin. Most of the time we had to unload the boat ourselves – I remember that there Mam and Dad would be shovelling the coal out, and the kids would wheel the barrows inside the factory, two kids to each barrow!

Then after the war, they said he had to have a motor boat, so we ended up with a motor and a butty. There were more of us children then, so we did need the extra cabin for everyone to sleep. Those boats had Bolinder engines, which used to shake them about something rotten! You'd have to keep an eye on them, because sometimes you'd find the planks springing, and that meant they'd leak when you were loaded – Dad would have to push clay in the gaps to stop them up. And we always had the stands and top planks collapsing; I can't tell you how many times that happened. That worried Dad, because if we were empty, that was our playground, in the empty hold! We'd often be running empty on the Duke's Cut (Bridgewater Canal), and he'd rig up a swing for us, using the short landing plank hung off the top plank with odd bits of rope.

Alice aged eight, on the 'Weston River' with a load of china clay

It was about that time, when I was very small, that Mam fell in a hole in the bank by Runcorn top lock, and hurt herself quite badly – there was a big hole in her leg, I remember. The lock-keeper was worse than useless; all he could say was that she shouldn't have been off the boat, only the captain should have been on the side – utter rubbish! How were we supposed to work boats like that? She never got any compensation, or even any help, she had to treat it herself, and go on working while it healed – and that took a long while.

And one day at Longport, my oldest brother Dennis who would have been about seven or eight was playing in a big pile of sand when he disappeared into it! He'd fallen into a hole underneath, and the sand collapsed around him – There was a bit of a panic, and everyone rushed up and helped to dig him out.

Alice with Lena Radford and Lassie on the Radford's butty Sunlight,
tied up at Longport in the Potteries

When I was small, about eight, I went with Mr and Mrs Radford on their boats for a while, because Mam and Dad had plenty of help, and they didn't have any children. They ran boats for a small factory in Stoke – they only had the one pair of boats, and all we did was to bring china clay from Weston Point to the factory. There's a picture of me, standing by the boats – the Radfords were quite posh, because they had a camera! I was with them a year or two, and then I went back with Mam and Dad.

One Christmas we were tied up at Barton Turn, outside the pub, and us kids decided to go carol-singing. The landlord invited us in, and we stood there in the pub singing away – I don't suppose we were that good, but the people must have taken sympathy on us, because we came out with sweets and stuff as well as quite a lot of money! Outside, a bunch of local kids were waiting for us, and gave us a hard time – I think they thought it was their privilege to sing in the pub. We managed to hang onto our money, only to have Dad take it off us when we told him. He controlled all the money we had – he was the one who got paid, Mam never earned a penny for the work she did, running the boat, keeping it and us clean and smart, or even shovelling coal!

We always went to the carnival at the top of Runcorn locks, every August Bank Holiday, and we used to earn by helping the pleasure boaters up the locks. We didn't usually get money, but they'd give us fruit and sweets, which we enjoyed much more, because we were allowed to keep them! We were at Runcorn once, when Dennis decided he wanted to go to the pictures. He stood on the anser pin, on the side of the butty, looking over in to the cabin to ask Mam if he could go. She handed him a big thick doorstep of a sandwich to keep him going, but just then his foot slipped and he ended up in the cut. The best thing was that when Dad fished him out, he still had hold of his sandwich!

Then around 1954, Mersey Weavers finished, so Dad had to find a new job. He went to British Waterways, ran a pair of boats for them from Anderton for a few years. Those were much smarter boats, built of steel rather than wood, and they were easier to keep clean and tidy. But then, it was about 1959, Waterways packed up in the potteries, and they had to come south. They were told to pick up a pair of boats at Glascote, that had been left there – they were loaded, so why they'd been left I don't know, but Mam and Dad had to bring them down to Bulls Bridge, and after that they ran out of there.

When that happened, both me and my brother George were already there. We'd come down with Mr and Mrs Jinks, working with them, and then I joined the Radfords again. I met them at Croxley, the Dickinsons paper mill. I went back with Mam and Dad when they came down, and then of course after a few years I was married to Les.

We didn't get much chance of schooling, and that's what I think I missed out on. If we hadn't finished boating when we did, I'd have left anyway when my own children were old enough to go to school, because I wanted them to have a decent education. Les did go to the school in an old boat at Bulls Bridge for a while, but he didn't like it and left as soon as he could! For me, schooling then meant getting a minibus which took five or six of us to an ordinary school near Brentford top

25

lock. We were kept segregated from the other kids, not just in lessons but at playtime too, in a separate yard cut off by a fence. The town kids would pick on us all the time, shouting names at us – they'd call us water gypsies, that was their favourite insult, and say we had fleas and things like that.

George and Annie Wain at Stoke Bruerne in the early 1950s

When I was a kid, I was very much the tom-boy, always in trouble. Mam was very safety-conscious, and would have us as toddlers in leather reins tethered to the cabin top – I think it was because she never learned to swim herself. I fell in the cut lots of times; I used to like to stand on the anser pin, a shackle on the side of the butty's stern, to look around, and slipped off it more than once! If I stepped onto it, Dad would tell me off:

'You'll be in again!'

The most common way for him to rescue me was to get hold of my thick head of hair. You not only had to get over the shock of falling in; you also received a clout off of Mam for falling in in the first place. It was for our own safety that she would lock us in the back cabin while she would fill or empty the locks. On one occasion, after tending to the lock, she noticed that I had gone missing. Both she and Dad thought I'd fallen in the cut, but instead they found me in the engine-room, sitting on the floor and playing, kicking the flywheel on the Bolinder engine while it was on. I had somehow climbed over the door at the back of the cabin into the engine 'ole; needless to say, I had a sore rear for a while.

Once when I was about six, we were working for Mersey Weavers, carrying chippings from Longport and buttying Uncle Bill and Auntie Lizzie (Dad's sister) on the Manchester Cut. I don't know what had gone wrong, but their butty began to sink, and she yelled out:

'We're going down!' Dad, who could swim, put our motor alongside, and dived into the cabin to save as much of their stuff as he could. I remember him describing how he found all their pots and pans floating in the water in there. The boat people were (and still are) a close community, and had to look out for each other.

When we went to school, some schools would segregate us from the town children, even at playtime. We had to eat our

27

meals in the classroom, away from the other children. Our time spent at school depended on the length of time our parents stayed in that particular area, whether it was waiting for orders or when the canal was frozen.

If a freeze was on for any length of time, jobs had to be found to compensate for the pay you lost – I can remember Dad and the other boaters being employed by British Waterways cutting hedges and cleaning the canals. For this kind of job, they were issued with donkey jackets and wellington boots, but when they returned to boating they had to hand them back and wear their own clothes. They got nothing for free, for their normal job!

At work during the freeze of 1963 – from the left, George Radford, Bert Wellington, Sam Horne, George Wain and Les Lapworth. On the Atherstone Pound, north of Suttons Stop.

Once the boats were loaded, we were excused from school and away we would go again on our journey with whatever cargo was to be transported. We didn't have many clothes, because of the limited amount of space in our living quarters, but we always had a set of best clothes, which we wore for special occasions. The rest of the time we were in our working clothes.

There were boarding schools to which some of the boat children were sent, my future husband being one of them, together with his sister and brother, but he hated it and only lasted a few years. Denis, Vera and I should have gone but we managed to escape the ordeal! The younger members of our family stayed in one such school in Birmingham for three or four years, only coming home in the school holidays. An old barge had been made into a schoolroom at Bulls Bridge, where we would wait for orders in the London area, and the boat children would attend there when their stay at the depot permitted.

The many hours we spent as children sitting and watching our parents working stood us in good stead for tending boats for ourselves, as we had to from an early age. After the age of five, we were considered old enough to be able to steer the boat; we used to stand on a stool so we could see over the cabin top, and we were told to hold the boat in the centre of the cut. We were taught how to use the boats and the locks to our advantage, so that no time was lost. While we were waiting for orders, we learned the crafts of the canals, fancy ropework and how to keep it looking as it should be. Some of the girls learned how to crochet, and we were shown the art of hanging up the decorative plates which hung in the back cabin. We used to sit and watch the traditional roses and castles being painted, and above all we learned how to clean the brasses.

The Fenny and the Titania loaded with coal in Braunston Top Lock, George Wain on the motor and Annie on the lockside. The other young man is Nicholas Hill.

In our leisure time, we would amuse ourselves as children do with anything we could lay our hands on. Fishing was a favourite, with a piece of string and a safety pin tied on the end, or a staple from an old book. We used to collect buckets of coal from the railway for the people in the houses so that we could save the pocket-money we earned to go to the pictures. Dad would play the accordion, and, as he could read, he would read out the newspapers to Mam and we would all listen. We had an old wireless which was powered by an accumulator, and we used to listen to The Archers, which was our favourite programme.

Trouble was always around the corner for me when I was a child. One day while sitting with my sister Anne, dangling a piece of string with a bent nail on the end in the cut we ended up falling out, and I hit her with the string. The nail caught her at the side of her eye, and when I saw blood running down her face it was time for me to run, anywhere but home, so I ended up at my cousin Phyllis's and stayed there for the rest of the day. When I eventually got home, Anne had been taken to have stitches in the wound and Mam and Dad's anger had worn off as they became increasingly worried about where I'd got to. On another occasion at Weston Point docks, Anne and I were playing 'follow the leader' along some wooden girders when Anne lost her balance and fell onto the concrete floor, breaking her front teeth. You can guess who was the leader, and who got the blame!

When my brother Dave was a baby I recall my Mam telling me to take him for a walk as he was very fractious for some reason. So off we went, with his sterry bottle with a teat on, filled with tea. Once we were out of sight I took the bottle and drank the lot – the tea for the baby always had a lot more sugar than we ever got, so it was a rare treat. When I returned home, Dave was still crying.

On another occasion, Dave being a bit older, I was lumbered with him again so off we went to the swings. It wasn't long before he fell off the swing, so back home we went with him crying again, but this time with a black eye and a lump on his head. After that Mam gave up and never sent me out with him again. When he was about five years old, and couldn't get his own way when he was in the back cabin while the boats were on the move, Dave would get back at Mam by hitting her on the toes with the poker as she stood on the footboard steering the butty.

Christmas must have been difficult for Mam and Dad, with a large family to support. We never had a Christmas tree, and the only decorations we could afford were paper-chains stuck up over the sidebed. But each of us would get one main present – a toy car, fire engine or a train set for the boys, and maybe a doll for the girls. One time I had a two-ended doll, with a white face one end and a black one the other, and a skirt which would turn inside out depending on which way up she was. You wouldn't be allowed anything like that nowadays! One very snowy Christmas, us three girls each had a Timex watch. We were very proud of these, but as you can imagine yours truly was the one who managed to scratch the face of hers, climbing up the bank. Scared of what Dad would say, I tried for ages to get Anne to swap with me, but without success.

We also got the traditional apple, tangerine and nuts in our stockings. One Christmas Eve when Vera and I had gone to bed – our bed being the floor under the cross-bed – we had a giggle when Dad came in to fill our stockings. Unfortunately, one of

32

the said stockings had a hole in the toe, and the surprise nuts were disappearing through it onto the cabin floor as soon as Dad put them in. Vera gave the game away by telling Dad about the hole, and was promptly told off for still being awake. Birthdays were never celebrated – not until I was courting did I receive regular birthday presents.

When our cargo was salt from Middlewich to Anderton, as children we had the job of filling and wheeling the barrow full of salt from the boats on the canal to the salt shoots, which were situated alongside the Anderton Lift. We would tip the salt onto the shoots, and the lads used to jump onto the shoots as well and have a slide down into the waiting river boats.

On occasions when we found old bikes in the cut, George and I would clean them up and use them as playthings. Punctured tyres were always a problem, so we filled the tyres with old rope, which proved a rather hard, bumpy ride, but we had some fun. One day we tried them down a hill at Croxley; I told George whatever happens, keep going straight, and what does he do but lose control of his bike which caused me to swerve and land on the ground at the wheels of a bus. And who should be on the bus but Dad. The bikes were taken away from us!

George nearly came to grief on another bike at Wheelock: Denis was giving him a ride on the crossbar, and the pair of them rode straight into the cut. Denis got out, but George was trapped, tangled up in the bike - luckily help was at hand, and he was soon rescued.

In those days it was not unusual for one or more members of a family to go off on a trip with another family who needed extra hands, as both Denis and I did. This also eased the sleeping arrangements on our boats. I spent some time with Mr and Mrs Dan Jinks, together with my brother George, and I kept my friend Agnes Radford company with her family on some of their journeys. Denis stayed at Middlewich with Mr and Mrs Jim Moors for nearly five years.

When we were old enough, Vera and I worked a pair of boats, Vera steering the motor while I was in control of the butty. This meant that, with Dad and Mam on one pair and Vera and I on another, we could earn twice as much to keep the family, and we had twice as much room to live in. Vera had the knack of starting up the old national engine on a cold morning, which as most people who have ever tried will know, is a job on its own. I can remember Dad almost in tears some mornings, trying to get his to start up! As a rule, Mam would cook breakfast for all of us, and ours she would leave on a lockgate for us to pick up as we passed through. Some mornings it would be stone cold, and on other mornings we would get there just in time to see a crow flying off with it. If we complained to Mam, we were told unsympathetically that if we hadn't been so far behind them, it wouldn't have happened.

We were stuck at Boxmoor once for quite a long time – the factories we delivered to had a full stock of coal, and didn't need any. I think it was the summer holiday period, when they were closed anyway. My sister Vera and I went to the labour exchange to see if we could get any help, and they told us there

Vera Wain with a new bike, in the 1960s.

were two jobs going at the local hospital, cleaning jobs. We had to ask Dad of course, but we wouldn't get any dole money while there were jobs we could do (not like these days!), so he said okay. We were there seven weeks; I was quite young, so I worked in the children's ward, while Vera, being older, cleaned an adult ward.

The money we earned was sent to Bulls Bridge for us, and of course they gave it to Dad! We worked from 6am to 2pm with just a cup of tea inside us, and then we would go home and help clean the boats before having our evening meal. All we saw was £2 10s (£2.50) for seven weeks work! This was at a time when the two of us were working one pair of boats, while Mam and Dad had another pair – but he was still the captain of all of them, so he was the one who got paid! It meant that, as a family, we could earn twice as much of course, running two pairs together like that.

The two of us stayed at the hospital all the time we were tied up, and at the end they asked us if we wanted to stay on. We could have lived in, as they had little flats we could have had, but by then both of us were engaged, me to Les and Vera to Ken Ward, so we elected to stay with the boats.

I worked in hospitals again later, after we'd left the boats. I was in an old folks' home for eleven and a half years, near where we lived in Coventry, and then I went to Walsgrave Hospital, and worked there for eight and a half years.

Les Lapworths's pair in Bushes Lock, Northchurch, Grand Union Canal, during the time he was courting Alice

BRANCHING OUT

As we got older, in our spare time a group of us would take an old record player and as many records as we could pool together into a nearby field and have a good time dancing. My friend Agnes was always popular, because she had many of the current records. I was thirteen years old when I first met a young lad from Nuneaton called Les Lapworth – he too was from a boating family, one of nine children. His family were based mainly at Bulls Bridge, which is near Southall in Middlesex, at the southern end of the Grand Union, and regularly carried

cargoes to and from Birmingham; from Longford they would load with coal and take it to Croxley Mill near Hemel Hempstead. His mother had died at the age of forty-four after giving birth to her ninth child.

Les Lapworth at 14, in the 'candlesticks', on the rebuilt northern Grand Union Canal.

REGISTRATION DISTRICT OF COVENTRY

13, *Little Park Street*.

Coventry.

24th. January, 1962

C. G. CAFFELLE
SUPERINTENDENT REGISTRAR

HOURS:—
MONDAY TO FRIDAY (INCLUSIVE) 9.30 A.M. TO 5 P.M.
SATURDAY 9.30 A.M. TO 12 NOON

Dear Sir and Madam,

I am writing to inform you that notice for marriage at The Register

Office

between   Mr. Leslie Lapworth

and   Miss Alice Wain

has this day been given ~~by~~ on behalf of your ~~son~~ daughter and that your consent to

the marriage has been received.

The time and date arranged for the ceremony is   10.20 a.m. on

Saturday 3rd. February, 1962.

~~No date has yet been fixed for the ceremony.~~

Yours faithfully,

C.G.Caffelle

Superintendent Registrar.

Mr. & Mrs. George Wain,

Finney 141, British Waterways,

Hawkesbury Stop, Coventry.

P.S.10305   43/4

*Alice and Les Lapworth's marriage consent certificate, addressed to
her father and mother*

She survived having a heart attack while delivering her son, but when she got back on board their boat 'Hampstead' she had another, from which she didn't survive. The boy, named Tony, was put up for adoption, and it was only in recent years, after my sister-in-law and I managed to trace him, have we had any contact with him.

Les at 15, dressed up after attending his mother's funeral

My first date with Les was a trip to the pictures while we were both tied at Sutton's Stop. He met me inside the picture hall, and sat at the back while I sat in the cheap seats at the front! We didn't see much of one another for long periods, because of our parents' work; it might be weeks before we met again. We began to get serious when I was fifteen years old, and by the time I was sixteen Les asked my Dad for permission for us to marry. My sister Vera had met her husband to be, Ken Ward, and she too was engaged by this time – my other sister, Ann, finally married into the same boating family when she met his brother Ted.

Les and I were about to be married, and so he set about acquiring a pair of boats through British Waterways at Bulls Bridge. Once that was organised he left the boats there and travelled back on the train to Coventry to his sister's, where he'd been living. We were married on February 3rd, 1962; Dad was with me, but Mam had to stay at home to look after the rest of the family.

Wedding Day! Les and Alice with their fathers, Tom Lapworth and George Wain, outside Coventry Register office

Our honeymoon was a trip from Brentford, full with barrels of lime juice destined for Roses factory at Boxmoor – and it wasn't without incident! Les had recently had a smallpox injection, and he had a really bad reaction to it; by the end of the trip he was very poorly, and the result was that he was ill in bed for a week, laid up under the doctor at Bulls Bridge.

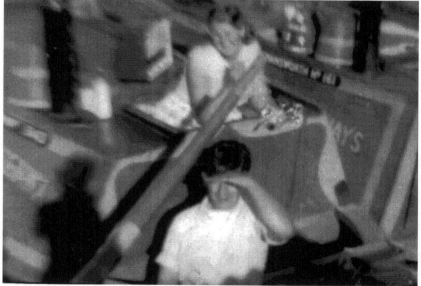

Alice in the hatches of the Satellite, with Les shading his eyes, tied up awaiting orders in the layby at Bulls Bridge

Once he was on the mend, we headed back to Brentford to load another cargo when disaster struck again! Les was chopping some wood with an axe, but he missed the wood and ended up less half a thumb. He got it bound up and carried on, but not content with that, later on the same trip he decided to jump off of the lockside onto the boat and landed awkwardly, twisting his knee. The result was that fluid built up around the knee causing it to swell – by the time we got back to Bulls Bridge it was so bad that the doctor had to cut his trousers away from the swelling before he could treat it. This time he was laid up for another week, one hand and the opposite leg all bound up. I was beginning to wonder what would happen next!

Stoke Bruerne, June 15th 1962 – Les and Alice Lapworth with their 'special trip' loaded with copper bars for Limehouse docks. George Wain, Alice's brother, on the lockside

Once he had recovered this time, we had regular trips from Bulls Bridge along the Grand Union to Birmingham. Some of the boats we knew then are now being used as houseboats or holiday boats – a few of the names I can bring to mind are Elstree, Andromeda, Hampstead, Fenny and Dee. I remember one special trip we had: There was a cargo of copper bars which we had to load at the top of Wolverhampton locks, to go to Limehouse Docks in London – they were going for export and we had to meet the ship in time for its sailing. My brother George came with us for the journey, and it took us less than a week to get there and back, which was good going. We got a nice bonus for that, so we splashed out on some new shoes!

On Tring Summit, another pair overtaking.
Photo by Les Lapworth

In those days time was everything to a boatman. If you let someone pass you it meant that they were at the depot before you, and if there was only one job available, they got it. You had no friends while you were working because of that rivalry – but in our leisure time we could relax and all have a bit of fun together.

Early Married life – Les and Alice at Bulls Bridge with a young Alan Wain

MY FAMILY

By this time I was three months pregnant with my first child. We carried on working until I was in my eighth month, but then I was forced to stop because I developed swollen ankles, so I rested until Denise was born on September 8th, 1962. After she arrived, we carried on working just as before, but of course I had also to tend to the baby, having to stop to breast feed or change her nappy when the need arose – Les always hated losing any time on a trip, for any reason, so as you can imagine, that caused a few problems.

Approaching Cosgrove from the Iron Trunk Aqueduct.
Photo by Les Lapworth

One time, we'd just come up through Hillmorton locks and were setting off along the pound. Denise was down in the cabin

45

and I knew she needed feeding, so I kept flashing the butty's headlamp to attract Les's attention. He saw me, but he took no notice, and eventually I got fed up with it and just left the tiller and went down into the cabin to look after her. The next thing, as you can imagine, the butty was up the bank:

'Why'd you do that?' was Les's question when he came back to see what was wrong, and he wasn't too pleased when I told him! As I say, he hated losing any time, and I was rather caught in the middle with a baby to look after.

On the North Oxford Canal, near Ansty, going to Suttons,
Mike and Janet Humphries in front.
Photo by Les lapworth

Another time we had a real row, going up Hatton locks – we'd gone about half way up, but once again she needed feeding, and he wouldn't stop so that I could look after her. I got so mad in the end that I walked off and left him! I went up all of two locks, but then I realised that I hadn't got anywhere to go, and I turned back. When I got back to the boats he was laughing:

'I knew you'd be back, 'cause you know I can't feed her!'

When we tied up at night, she would need feeding, changing and bathing again, just like any other baby, and her nappies would need washing. These chores would go on until eleven or twelve at night – and we'd be up at five the next morning again!

Above Cowley Lock, Alice just visible on the Capella

Of course, everything that went wrong on the boats was my fault! One day, Les was trying to show off, turning the pair out of the layby at Bulls Bridge in one go. He wound the engine up a bit too much and broke the snatcher, but it was still my fault!

Les and Johnny Best leaving Dudswell top lock on a trip with two single motor loads.

Les always liked his pint of a night, after we'd tied up. I would stay on the boats – I wasn't one for the pub even before Denise was born, and afterwards I had to look after her anyway. I didn't like the dark, and some of the places we stopped were really very dark and quite unpleasant – one night, we'd tied by the Black Boy, below the locks at Knowle, where it was very black. I was really unhappy there on my own until Les came back. Then another time we stopped at the top of Hatton, where the cut goes into that cutting. It was so black and horrible there, but Les insisted on walking across the fields to the pub. All of a sudden, the butty rocked and the doors flew open; a foot appeared on the step, and the tale of a coat I didn't recognise. I let out a yell and leapt into the bed-hole, only for Les to come and give me a good shake to calm me down and tell me 'it's only me!' He'd got a new coat from somewhere – and he gave me such a scare!

Another time he gave me a scare was once when the butty was really heavily loaded, going up from Brentford. On the deep water down that end of the cut, he set off hell for leather, going so fast that the butty was being pulled down and nearly swamped. I yelled at him to slow down, but he didn't take any notice! We didn't sink, but it did give me a fright.

Too fast and too heavy! See above.
Photo by Les Lapworth (!)

One time we were laid up at Bulls Bridge with no loads to be had for a few days. My sister Ann was there too, with her husband Ted Ward, and the four of us just went for a trip, for the fun of it! The weather was lovely, and we really enjoyed ourselves.

Holiday Snap! Alice on the motor with Les relaxing on the cabintop, with Ted and Ann Ward on the butty, just above Winkwell locks.

We used to see holiday boats about quite often, and they could be a real nuisance sometimes. They wouldn't listen to us, wouldn't do whatever we asked, which used to get us both in trouble! We'd sometimes need them to go the other side of us, so our loaded boats could have the deeper water, but they'd insist on going where they'd been told they should, and then we'd both end up stuck. The boats then were mostly fibreglass cruisers, or wooden ones, old lifeboats and the like, and you were scared of hitting them with big steel boats like ours; I ran into one, one night in the dark! It had come adrift, and the wash from the motor sucked it out, right in front of the butty, and of course I couldn't stop, and didn't have the time or the room go around it. I don't know if we sunk it, we didn't stop to find out!

The folks on those boats didn't have any time for us. They didn't seem to understand that boating was our living, our way of life; like I say, they wouldn't listen to advice. They treated us like lepers, most of the time, thought they were better than us because they had homes on the bank – it was the same old 'dirty boatees' attitude that we got from all the town people, as we called them, they thought of us as gypsies. All lot of the time, if you needed one, even the doctors wouldn't come out to the boats!

And although things have changed quite a bit, some people still have that idea of us. We were tied up at the bottom of Napton once, by the pub there, with our pleasure boat, the Jupiter. Les was in the pub, and I was leaning on the side of the boat in the evening sunshine, when this couple came walking by. They stopped to talk, looking at the boat, and the lady started going on about how did the old boat people ever manage in their little cabins? I didn't let on we were boaters, and she was saying wherever did they go to the toilet? So I suggested they mostly had porta-pottis, which we did, at least in the later days, but she said:

'Oh no, I don't think so! And anyway, they were much too dirty to have things like that!' I don't know if my expression gave me away, but her husband asked;

'Were you off the boats?' So I told him yes I was – she got quite embarrassed, but I told them a bit about how life had really been, and then he said:

'You should write a book about it!'

Alice's sister Ann Ward, the famous Grove Park Bridge on the Grand Union Canal in the background.

We spent that last Christmas at Sutton's. On Christmas Day, Les went off with his mate Abel Beechey for a drink in the Greyhound; he said he wouldn't be too long, but I knew better! They stayed there until closing time in the middle of the afternoon, and even then came out of the pub each carrying a two-gallon watercan full of beer. They went off to one of the row of cottages there with other friends to drink it, and then when they eventually emerged again, the two of them had a bet that they could walk a straight line along the bank, back to the boats. Les actually managed it, but Abel was all over the place!

That was the winter of the big freeze. We were frozen in at Sutton's, with a load of coal that was destined for Dickinson's mill at Apsley. We got there in the end, but when Les eventually got to Bulls Bridge and went to the office to settle up, they told him it was all finished. Trading on the canals had come to an end, and with it came the end of an era.

Although I think we knew that the end was going to come, when it did we were still gutted. A lot of the boat people were allowed to live on the boats which they had worked until they could find alternative accommodation, and where possible, another way to earn a living. Many of the boat people found it very difficult to adapt to a new way of life; some succeeded, but many found that with no education life from then on would be even more of a struggle, having to live alongside the 'people in the houses' as they were known to us.

*Leaving the boats. Les holding Denise on the day he and Alice
moved into the caravan*

Denise was eight months old by now; we lived on board the
Satellite and the Elstree at Sutton's for six months, during which
time Les found employment as a labourer on a building site. He
couldn't settle at this, and moved on to a job in a factory, but he
couldn't get on with this either. Eventually, he wound up at
Readymix Concrete, which seemed to suit him much better. We

did manage to save up some money, and with this we bought a new caravan, which we lived in for the next five years.

My Mum and Dad stayed on the boats. Dad was getting near retirement anyway, and they didn't know any other life, he couldn't have found a job on the bank. He went to Willow Wren, but didn't stay very long – the boats weren't in very good shape, and the work was difficult, never knowing where you'd be sent next. He gave it up, and they went back to Runcorn and lived in the house, but his health suffered. He never really recovered from the loss of his way of life.

On June 10th, 1964, my elder son Leslie was born. When Denise and Leslie were old enough to go to school, both Les and I decided that we should try to learn to read and write, for the children's sake. So we signed on at the local night school, where the teacher was amazed at how we had coped not being able to read or write, especially when I went shopping for food! Les learned a lot quicker than I did – I got by, but I found it a real struggle, although I am reaping the rewards because now I am able to read a book. I will admit though that my spelling leaves a lot to be desired – but old as I am, I'm still learning, sounding out words until they make sense.

When Les and I were going to evening classes, to learn to read and write, I would sometimes leave notes for him in the house. My writing is still very bad – you'd never be able to understand it! – but Les could, of course. He'd make fun of me, pretending that I'd written swear words in these notes, and wind me up about being able to write those when I couldn't write other things!

Les and Alice on Holiday in Rhyl, North Wales, with Denise and Leslie in 1968.

Rhyl again – Les with George Carter, another ex-boatman, and Denise in the background.

His writing was always much better than mine – he'd had some time in school when he was younger, and picked it up much quicker than I did once we decided to try to learn, when the children were going to school. And after five years in the caravan, at last we'd saved up enough to buy a cosy little house in Alderman's Green, in Coventry, close to the canal and not far from Sutton's Stop.

While Les was still working for Readymix, in February 1977, our third child was born – thirteen years after the last one! Lee came along on the 24th of that month. He was about five or six when, with the experience he'd gained from working at Readymix, Les decided to set up his own business, making and

Christening Day! Proud parents Les and Alice with baby Lee.

building prefabricated concrete garages. He went into partnership with another fellow, who luckily did most of the paperwork, and it all went very well. After a few years, the other man wanted to pack up and so Les bought him out, and started going to night school to learn about running a business. It's still going now, although since Les passed on it's being run by young Les and Denise.

Lee as a toddler enjoying a happy moment with his father

For many years we spent our leisure time touring the canals on our own narrowboat, Jupiter. We had to smile, watching how some of the present-day owners of the old working boats tried to manoeuvre them out of tight corners or around bends – but more than that, when they tried to tell us how it should be done!

One time, boating in the Jupiter, we had an experience which was both heartening and upsetting at the same time. We were near Salford Turn, where the Birmingham & Fazeley

Canal and the Tame Valley Canal meet, and we picked up a set of bedsprings on the propeller, which brought us to a halt right under a bridge. It just happened that the local fire brigade were parked on the bridge, testing their pumps, and some of the firemen came down to help when they saw our predicament. They got the springs off for us, and then wouldn't take any money for their efforts – but I did make them a cup of tea! It was while we were chatting that they told us they had been the crew who had been called out to an accident on the canal – they had had the horrible task of cutting the body of a school-teacher out of the propeller after she had fallen overboard during a trip with a lot of the schoolchildren on board.

In later life – Les Lapworth with his sons, Lee on the left and Leslie on the right

We would meet up with various friends and members of our families at the annual boat rallies in places like Middlewich, Dudley, Windmill End, Braunston, and many more. Old habits die hard, and whenever he got the chance, Les would like to steer one of the old boats. You'd see him at most of the rallies, whenever he could leaning on the tiller of one of the many working boats. It was always a chance to meet some of the boat people we hadn't seen for many a year, to exchange stories and bits of news, and to have a laugh remembering some of the more amusing incidents that had cropped up when we were boating.

Les with Ron Withey on one of the 'Jam 'Ole runs' in the 1990s.

Les and another old boatman, Ron Withey, took part a number of times in what is called the 'Jam 'Ole Run', which was the journey his old friend Ernie Kendall used to make carrying coal from Warwickshire to the jam factory of Kearley and Tonge's near Bull's Bridge, at Southall in London. That was the last long-distance carrying job on the canal, and they've re-enacted it more than once now – videos have been made of the event, and the proceeds are going to the restoration of some of the boats which were involved.

On the River Severn at Gloucester – from the left:
Joe Safe, Les, Ron Withey and Andrew Burge.

LIFE TODAY

Les started feeling unwell in 2004, and he couldn't seem to get any better; he just got worse and worse, and in the end he died in the September. And as time goes by, we seem to hear all too often of the sad passing of friends and family members. My Dad's youngest brother Jim lost his battle against cancer in November 1999, but his boat, the old icebreaker Shackleton, can still be seen touring the canals with his wife Mary on board, and their son Jim at the tiller.

Annie Wain back on the boats at Sheffield in 1991. The motor in the background is her son George's England.

Two of my brothers still own boats – George has the England, and Ray owns the motorised butty Titania. John is still involved with boats too – he fits them out for Les Wilson at his yard on the North Oxford Canal. Our Mam, Annie, died in 2007 at the grand age of 86; she'd born thirteen children in all, and must have been saddened when my brother Dennis died nine months before she did. And my youngest brother Alan died just last year, in 2009.

I still live in the house we bought all those years ago, in Alderman's Green, and I'm a proud grandma too – five grandchildren so far! Denise's son David is 28 now; Leslie has two children, his son Wain is 21, and his daughter Bailey is 20. And now Lee has two youngsters as well – Louis is 7, and his sister Gracie is 4. I like to go down to the canal from time to time, and still like to visit the boat rallies even though it isn't by boat any more. As I travel around, I can see that all the old familiar landmarks are changing, too. Factories, pubs and warehouses are being knocked down, and the depots from which we used to work, once so full of hustle and bustle, now lie ghostly silent and derelict. New Marinas are springing up everywhere.

So many of the locks and pounds as we knew them are being known now by different names – I can still recall some of the Cheshire locks from Middlewich to Harecastle Tunnel, as we used to know them:

Big Lock, Middlewich Three, Kings Lock, Joe Lowes, Booth Lane Three, Crows Nest, Willock Two, Clock Lock, Shithouse Lock, Hassle Green Two, Hassle Green Single, Mortar Board Two, Bottom-o-New'uns Three, Church Two, Church Pound, Red Bull Two, Lime Kiln Lock (where you could get clean water), Plants Lock, and then the tunnel. I know I've missed a few along the line, but I'm sure someone will remind me of them!

As my journey takes me past Westport Lake, Longport, where Dad's dream began, I try to picture how it was in those days. Sadly only pleasure boats pass by now, with perhaps an occasional working boat, the sound of its engine echoing as it passes and fades into the distance.

Where has it all gone?

Still boating! Alice enjoys her occasional visits to canal events, and she is seen here steering the Narrowboat Trust's butty Brighton at the annual Braunston Historic Boat Show in 2011.
Photo courtesy of Tim Coghlan.

APPENDIX:

Some Notes Written by Les Lapworth, and photographs from his collection:

One of my earliest memories when I was a young boy living on the canals is still vivid in my mind. I was about four or five years old at the time and my mother had taken me out of the cabin and sat me on the cabin top which the boat people called the slide so that I could enjoy the scenery. At the time we were travelling along one of the cleaner and more pleasant stretches of the canals known as the Paddington Arm in London. It was early morning possibly 7.30 because we had to be at our destination the Greenford Works by eight o'clock to unload our cargo of coal. Suddenly I started screaming and I felt a pain in my arm. The noise startled my mother and she found a pellet had marked my skin, she shouted 'Tom! Tom! Someone has shot at Leslie.'

My father stopped the motor boat and came back to the butty, which was the name we gave to the second boat. When my father saw what had happened he scaled off the boat; this meant using a pole to catapult himself from the cabin top onto the towpath, and went to the factory from which my mother thought the pellet had come. He spoke to the man in charge who made enquiries and the culprit was found. My father led him back to the boats to show him what he had done and pointed out that it could have been far worse. He was very apologetic, and the reason I remember it so clearly is because the man gave me ten shillings!

The layby at Bulls Bridge – Phyllis Lapworth peeling the potatoes with her son Ron on the ropes. A cheeky Les is in the hatches of the motor boat.

I remember when I was about ten years old my father decided it was time I went to school. It was agreed that I should go to Birches Green School in Birmingham which was recommended by British Waterways, the firm my father worked for. Like the other children whose parents worked on the canals I was to be a boarder. At school I was under the care of Mrs Harper who was very understanding. She realised that I was behind the other children of my age but she never let them discover this, something for which I was most grateful. She willingly gave up her breaks and time after school to raise the standard of my work. When I was given the chance to move up to a higher class I chose to stay with Mrs Harper.

Les's grandparents – his grandfather Mr Wilson on the left, and grandma Wilson on the right in the hat

Les's mother Phyllis, foreground in the coat, at a Christmas function for boater's children in the early 1950s.

*While he was courting Alice, Les Lapworth ran a pair of boats with
another young unmarried boatman. They are seen here heading north,
above Northchurch Lock on the Grand Union Canal.*
Photo by Les Lapworth

On the same trip, with empty boats now, Les plans on some sunbathing!

POSTSCRIPT

By Geoffrey Lewis

I first met Alice Lapworth at the Braunston Historic Boat gathering some years ago. I had known Les, in the fashion of boaters, as someone I would see around 'the cut', someone to tip your hat to with the usual ''Ow d'yeh do?' as we passed, either on the stern of the Jupiter or perhaps steering an ex-working boat at Braunston or another canal event. It was during that first meeting that she mentioned to me that she had had a single short book produced about her life, some years earlier, as a present for Les on his sixtieth birthday.

By the time we met, he had sadly died, but she was interested in having that book republished as something for a wider audience. We got to talking – and this volume is the result! I have, over some two years or more, spent many enjoyable hours in Alice's company, listening to her reminiscences of her life on the boats, both as a child with her parents and later with Les, and those chats have enabled me to add significantly to the content of this book. She has also allowed me access to her private photograph collection, from which all the pictures included here are taken. And I am now proud to count Alice among my circle of true friends.

This book is based very much upon that earlier one-off copy which I have been privileged to borrow. Alice is keen to acknowledge the help that she received then from Beryl England and her husband Bob, who did much of the work of putting it all together. I too would offer them my thanks – that framework saved me an enormous amount of time! I have tried to insert the new material as best I could in chronological order; and I have tried all through to keep Alice's

73

own words, so that it speaks with her voice and not mine. I know there are anomalies – I have not tried to iron them out! But I think her story speaks for itself, and paints in the mind of the reader a very clear and captivating picture of the life of a boating family in the days when the canals were still fulfilling their intended purpose.

I hope that this book will give you as much pleasure in the reading of it as it did me in the collation and preparation.

Geoffrey Lewis
January 2012

Canal Books from SGM Publishing:
Historical Novels by Geoffrey Lewis

The Michael Baker trilogy is set around Britain's Canals in the days of the commercial carrying trade. Beginning at the start of the Second World War, the story carries us through into the 1950s, telling of the joys and sorrows, the triumphs and tragedies of the working boat people, relating a way of life that is now gone forever. Meticulously researched and told with warmth and sympathy by a true canal enthusiast.

'Accurately drawn from his own experience over many years'
    Martin Ludgate, Canal Boat Magazine
'It is a tale to melt all hearts'
    Stan Holland, Canals & Rivers Magazine

www.sgmpublishing.co.uk

More of Geoffrey Lewis' Canal Fiction:

***Starlight** is a poignant tale of schoolboy friendship and loyalty, set alongside the Oxford Canal in 1955. It tells of one boy's discovery of the world of the waterways with his new friend, the local lock-keeper's son.*

'A beautiful tale, beautifully told'
Roger Wickham, Amherst Publishing

*Geoffrey Lewis' **Jess Carter** stories are delightful, historically truthful canal-set tales for the younger reader, aged from ten to around a hundred.*

Set on the unusual tanker narrowboats of Thomas Clayton Ltd, in the months immediately before World War II, they too paint a realistic picture of the lives of the boating people.

The first book tells of a journey with a horse-drawn boat to Ellesmere Port in Cheshire; the second describes the adventures of Jess and Luke Kain as they bring their new motor-boat from Uxbridge to Birmingham.

76